DOGS

Ben Wicks

London-born Ben Wicks left school at fourteen to embark on a varied career as barrow boy, clog-maker, electrician's mate, infantryman and glider pilot in the army, and clarinet player aboard the *Queen Elizabeth*. He emigrated to Canada in 1957 where he worked as a window cleaner, prison warder, musician and milkman before finally trying his hand at cartooning.

In addition to writing his bestselling books and preparing his daily cartoon features, Wicks appears on Canadian television whenever his dog Rosie lets him.

DOGS

Ben Wicks

A STAR BOOK
Published by
the Paperback Division of
W.H. ALLEN & Co. PLC

A Star Book

Published in 1984
by the Paperback Division of
W. H. Allen & Co. PLC
44 Hill Street, London W1X 8LB

First published in Canada by McClelland and Stewart Limited, 1983

Printed in Great Britain by
Cox & Wyman Ltd, Reading

ISBN 0 352 31549 0

Contents

Introduction

Our dog is named Rosie.
She came to us as a replacement for two cats.
These cats had been asked to leave the house
when it was found that my youngest daughter
was allergic to cats.
Unfortunately my youngest
daughter
was not allergic to Rosie.
Now, after seven years
of
yelling, screaming, and shouting
we are
sufficiently
trained to do
whatever Rosie wants.
For this reason
I am in a position
to write a book about
the many Rosies sharing
(and in many cases ruling)
this world of *ours.*
It is my earnest
desire that those planning
to become Rosie owners will
be forewarned.

Those suffering souls who have taken up this book
with four muddy Rosie paws already padding around the
house will be comforted in the knowledge that they
are not alone.

Ben Wicks
Toronto, Canada
1983

THIS BOOK
IS DEDICATED
TO ROSIE

What is a Dog?

A dog is man's best friend (which
does not say much for his others).
A dog has four legs, two ears,
two eyes, a tail, and a wet nose.
A dog can hear a fridge door
opening from the end of
the street.
He will bring slippers or a
newspaper when he is asked.
Or an old bone when he is not.
A dog will wag his tail when
you praise him.
And wag his tail when you scold him.
A dog will drive you crazy
most
of the time.
And love you all of the time.
A dog is a dog.

The Origin of the Species

Many experts say
that the dog
was around before
Adam and Eve.
Rubbish.
God had enough trouble
making something
with two legs
without
messing about
trying to make
something with
four.

Well then, where did dogs come from?

A tricky question.
Man can look back
through the ages and see
a lumbering oaf covered in hair.
The dog has no such
family portraits.
All we know for sure
is that he was nowhere to be seen
when Adam and Eve were fooling around
in the garden.
If he had been, the apple
would have been eaten long before
Adam could get a bite.

The dog first appeared during the age of the dinosaurs. With its two little legs in the front and two big ones at the back, the tyrannosaurus had the makings of a dog.

Gradually the two big legs at the back began to wear down. This is no surprise since these were the legs doing all the work.

A million years or so later, these legs had worn down so much that the animal found its two front legs touched the ground.

The dog had arrived.

30,000,000 YEARS
10,000,000 YEARS
50,000,000 YEARS
5 YEARS

But an incredible change
had taken place.
From the 45-foot-long
giant dogasaurus
he was down to a
miserable three feet.
(Food had not been
plentiful.)

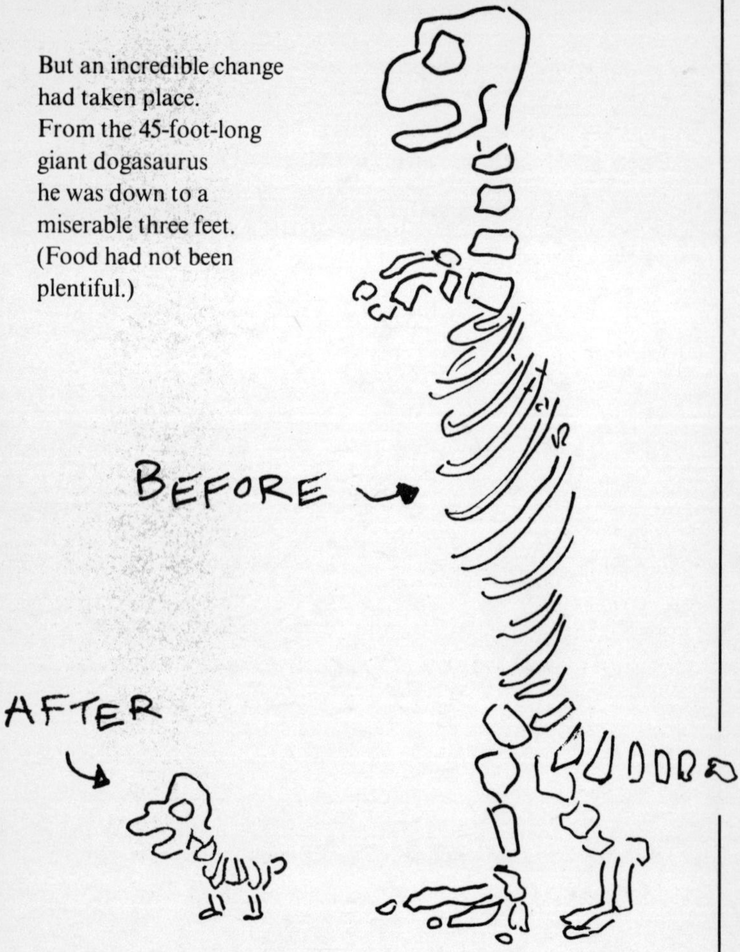

And since the rule of the time was
first come
first served,
to survive was not easy.

Of all the animals, it seemed the human was making out the best – running, screaming, and flinging stones at anything that moved. Obviously, standing still was the only way to a long and fruitful life.
When this became very boring, the dog decided to do what any clear thinking warrior in the field would do.
Join the side of the strong.
Soon he was creeping into caves licking the first filthy hand he could find.
Man began to look at the creature with new interest.
What was this dog-animal that licked the hand of man without eating it?

One day, a cave-man, brighter than the others, made a discovery: dog had two more legs than man.

Here was the answer to a major problem.
All too long man had suffered the indignity of arriving at a kill long after the rest of the jungle had licked their chops and gone for a nap.

Dog was the way to get off a diet of bones and feathers and into fresh meat.
Dog would be man's legs.

As an added plus dog would be man's
eyes and ears during danger.
Each time a sabre-tooth tiger poked its
head into the cave, dog would bark.
Thus man learned when
to go to the front door and when
it was better to send someone else.
Man had found a friend.

By the time the Pharoahs were building
pyramids and marrying their sisters,
the dog had become a household hieroglyph.
It was impossible to write a
sentence without the shape of a dog
in it. They were everywhere.
Painted dogs with round faces, sculpted dogs with square faces, chiselled dogs with long faces, and dogs on parchment with no faces.

But we mustn't leap to the conclusion that this is the way dogs looked during this period. Egyptian artists were incredibly bad. One look at the way they drew people tells us that drawing a proper dog was too much for them.

But lousy artists or not,
the Egyptians loved their dogs.
So much so that even in death they
refused to be parted from Fido.
Fido remained at the feet of his human
– mummified.
Since the dogs of this world enjoy life as much
as anyone else, this idea was not appealing.
It's one thing to wrap it up after you've sucked
in your last breath.
It's quite another when you have
thousands of breaths still to go.
So the job was done as painlessly as possible.

1
BANDAGE
2
PASTE
3
BALL
4

And thus man and dog have come
down through the ages.
Wherever man has gone, the dog has been
at his side (or feet).

So much for where the dog came from.
Where is it going?
If the answer is "your house" then you'll need to
know a lot more about it than the shape of its
family tree.

Choosing a Dog

What dog should I buy?
That depends on what you want to do with it.
All dogs do absolutely nothing
unless
encouraged.
If you don't want them to do much
the answer is simple.
Any dog.
If, however, you want a
dog to be useful,
you'll be happy to know
that there are breeds
willing to undertake almost any
chore.

Types of Dogs

Sporting Dogs

For a dog that is guaranteed to fetch almost anything you can kill, consider the retriever.

(1) Speed is not essential: what-
ever it is is already dead and not
about to go anywhere.

(2) No teeth is a definite plus:
after a successful
shot straight between the eyes there is nothing more
disappointing than to get back nothing
but a handful of
feathers.

(3) Must be a good pointer.
Why this is I do not know.
If you are aiming a rifle at something
you shouldn't need a dog
to point its nose and tail.
It's just an ego trip for the dog.

(4) Must be able to swim: everything
a hunter hits ends up in water.
Deep water.

A Few Pointers:

To Be Retrieved	Kind of Dog
DUCK	Likes water and icy rain. Hates the taste of duck.
RABBIT	Enjoys dark narrow corridors and crawling on its stomach. Hates *Watership Down.*
PARTRIDGE	Bird watcher.
MOOSE	Large.

The Husky

You'll be wanting more than one.
How many will depend on your size.
Your dogs will be pulling
you and a nasty great sleigh.
Don't forget to test their hearing.
Screaming "mush"
to a set of deaf dogs
could leave you frozen solid in no time.
Huskies also double as a door for your
igloo so don't forget to take along the
measurements of your
igloo tunnel.
The wrong size dog could get stuck in
the tunnel. This is bad for the dog and not all
that great for you.
Especially if you're on the inside.
Be sure that the huskies you buy are prepared
to stand up to a ten-foot polar bear.

Here's a simple test. First you'll need
the help of the pet-shop owner.
Climb up on his shoulders.
Now wave your arms and growl.
Is the dog cowering in the corner?
This is not the dog for you.
Has the dog immediately attacked
the pet shop-owner's legs?
This is the dog for you.
When you can look on safely as your dog
chases a hungry polar bear across the Arctic wastes,
you will relish the memory of deciding to buy
this most noble canine.
If there's no polar bear in sight, you may also relish the dog.
One other thing.
If you live in a warm climate and are concerned
about taking such a dog out of its natural environment,
don't be.
If he feels homesick, there's always the freezer.

The Hound

There are two types.
Those that smell and those that see.
Which one you buy depends on what you need it for.

For a prison warden I would recommend a smeller.
Most prisoners nip over the wall after dark.
There's not much point in buying a dog with 20/20 vision if it's too dark for it to see.
A smeller, however, will have its nose to the ground and be away like a racehorse regardless of the dark.
The dog will be chasing a human who is running.
And has a head start.
So don't pick a hound with little legs.

Make sure that he enjoys the water.
Most escaped prisoners watch enough TV
to know that even the best smeller
is beat once the track is lying under water.
These cads with their numbered shirts
usually make for the nearest river and
splash their way downstream to freedom.
No sweat.
Buy two dogs.
One for downstream and one for up.
If both have good hearing and a liking
for the water you'll soon have your escapee
treed like a possum.

The Working Dog

Dogs want to please.
It's the fastest way to get what they want.
Some do tricks.
Others shake hands.
And others work.

Desperate for a pat on the head, these unsung blue-collar workers of the canine community are ready to lift a bale and tote a barge at the slightest lift of their master's hand.
Here are a few:

Milk-Cart Puller

Rare in these days of the supermarket, the milk-cart dog can still be seen in Europe making its way through the cobbled streets.
A happy-go-lucky dog that likes nothing more than giving free rides to the village children after the milk is delivered.
If this dog suits your business plans, look at its feet.
The flatter the better.
One slip on the cobbled streets and it could be game over.
While you stand there crying over it, you could be the laugh laugh of Baden Baden.

The Police Dog

If you're a believer in law and order,
the police dog is your cup of tea.
(Many of my friends own one just to show whose side
they're on when they're stopped for speeding.
"Hi there, Officer. I have one of your buddies in the
car. Say hello to the nice officer, Hercules.")
Used mainly to keep demonstrators in line.
Ideal for the job since they don't vote.
They don't care which side they bite.
You'll need one with long teeth.
The longer the better.
Their bark *may* be worse than their bite,
but who wants to find out?

The Doberman

Vicious.
Will bite anyone including its master.
Would have been destroyed
years ago, but nobody has
had the guts to get close
enough to do the job.

The Collie

Best known for its movie role as Lassie.
Gentle, kind, tolerant,
mild, patient, and
compassionate.
Except to sheep.

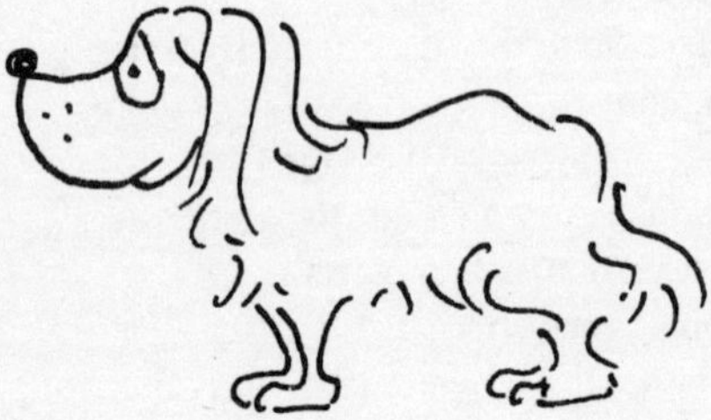

The Alpine Patrol Dog

The St. Bernard is a huge dog with a heart of gold.
Ready to climb the highest mountain and burrow its
way through the deepest snow in order to rescue man.

A man whose only reason for climbing the mountain
in the first place was that it is there.
Luckily for the man, so is the St. Bernard.
Where there's a cry for help, he is there.
One important point when buying a St. Bernard.
Get a teetotaller.

The Terrier

Bred to go down holes.
Once in the hole it'll
fight whatever it was that
went down the hole
before it.
If you have a hole that you
want something to go down,
this is the dog for you.

The Message Carrier

Although pigeons are the better known carriers of messages
no one has ever stopped to ask themselves, "What if the message
is too long to tie to the pigeon's foot?"
Here is where we find our ever-faithful friend.
The dog.
With a long history of bravery in the field of battle,
this dog may again save the day.
Trapped, as you may very well be, in a nuclear fall-out shelter,
how better to send word of your whereabouts?
With its natural homing instinct, the message-
carrying dog will find its way back to you
without fail.
However, there is one minor problem:
how to get the dog to leave home in the first place.
Many message-dog owners claim that they have overcome this
problem.
They take the dog to whoever the message is
for and watch with pride as the dog
races off home with the answer.

The Look-Alike

The one drawback to being a dog
is that you do not have any say
in who becomes your owner.
Many a miniature dog faces the daily embarrassment of walking
the streets with an oversized owner. Many a Great Dane
hangs its head in shame as it crosses the park dragging
a less than great human.
For upwardly mobile dogs,
a look-alike owner is ideal.
Fortunately, it's just a matter of time.
Eventually all owners look like their dogs.
The dog doesn't care what
he looks like.
He's going to find
friends in the park
if he looks like a cross between
a duck-billed platypus and a goat.

This is not the case
with the human.
In this vain world the
human is constantly told that
if he doesn't have the right
image, he'll never make it.

So before you buy your dog take a good look
in the mirror.
What do you look like?
I'm not suggesting
that you buy a dog that looked like you did
as a baby. Look for one that has a good chance
of moulding its face into yours as you stumble
side by side into life's setting sun.

You'll need a very healthy dog.
Remember – the longer you have him the more he
will grow to look like you.
You're living in the same house,
eating the same food (most of the time),
drinking the same chemical-filled water,
and braving the same elements.
Why shouldn't you look alike?

However, you can help Mother Nature.
At least give the dog you're about to buy
a sporting chance of becoming a twin without
having to resort to drastic measures.

Buying A Dog

These are two kinds of dogs.
One is a pure bred and one isn't.
The Isn't is what we are going to deal with first.

First, they're cheap. In most cases free, gladly given away by owners who want to get back to a normal life.

The Isn't comes in all shapes and sizes . . . all odd.

ISN'TS

Where To Find It:

An Isn't can be found in one of two places.
1. On your front lawn.
2. In the pound.

On Your Front Lawn

This dog will be owned by a neighbour across the street.
He has an immaculate lawn and wishes to keep it that way.
If you take his dog, you will soon have the neighbour rapping on your door.
He is afraid that you are about to train his dog to do to his front lawn what he has trained it to do to yours.

The Pound

Most of the dogs
are inches away from
the great upstairs.
They will spend the
rest of their days
being grateful
to you for having
pulled them from
the jaws of death.

This servile gratitude
should be encouraged,
particularly when complete
obedience
is called for:
"Do that once more and you'll go
back where you came from."

Threatening a dog
that you've stolen off
the street may just encourage
his bad behaviour.
The home he came from
may have been much better than yours.

The pound is noisy, smelly, and full of dogs.
You are there to pick a dog. Not a collie, Not a poodle.
A dog.
And the dogs know this.
This could be their big chance.
They will do almost anything
to make you choose them.
Don't be fooled.
A dog in the pound may not be
the same dog in your house.

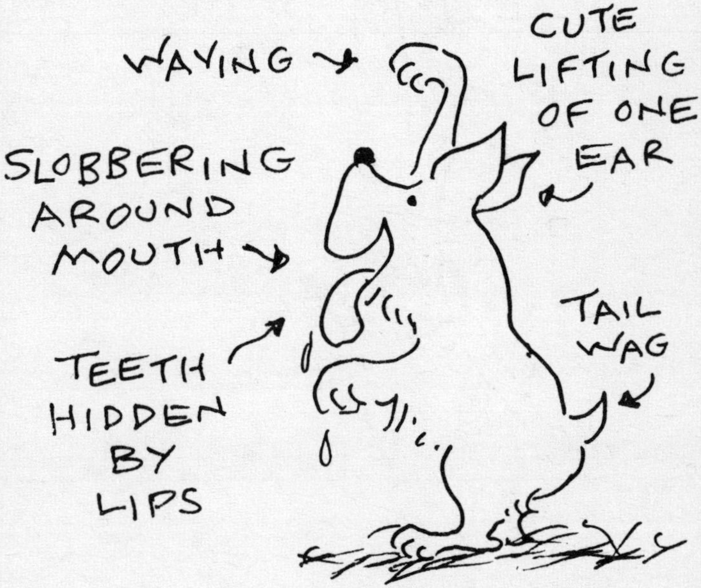

Many of them will attempt to lick
your hand.
This is a ploy used by dogs to hide the
fact that they have teeth.
Others will stand with
legs crossed until you have
left the building.

A tail that wags is good. So is a nose that is cold
and wet.

Ignore the advice of the person in charge of the pound.
They will be attempting to get rid of the
dog that is giving them the most trouble.

Once you have decided on the dog that you feel
will give you the least problems
have him released from his pen.
Many dogs, finding freedom suddenly,
lose all control,
knocking to the ground all
who stand in their way.

Let him go.
He'll be picked off the street again soon.
You want a calmer dog anyway.
Pick one up and cradle him in your arms,
belly up and feet in the air.
This will tell you if your dog is too big to pick
up and cradle in your arms.
Stare him in the eye.
Call him by the name you have chosen for him.
If he falls out of your arms laughing,
you can revert to the old
stand-bys: Rover, Fido, or Spot.

If he is still on his back, note his
responses.
The following chart should help:

Response	*Result*
Lies there doing nothing.	Could be dead. Check for breathing.
Whines and wriggles.	Needs the washroom.
Licks hand and face.	Good one.

How is his hearing?
Call to the dog.

Response	*Result*
Does nothing.	Deaf.
Lifts its head.	Deaf but reads lips.
Jumps into your arms.	Good one.

One other thing.

You may feel that you are doing the pound a favour by taking this creature off their hands. They don't. They expect to be paid. They claim it's to cover the cost of the shots they give the dog before you leave.

These shots are to ensure that he won't take with him the million diseases carried by other dogs in the pound.

Many feel that a dog from the pound is like
a baby from the church steps.
These folks are looking
for a different kind of dog.
Dogs that are guaranteed to play with children
and rip an intruder into little pieces.
Animals that immediately sit when told,
and kill on command.
Dogs that shake hands and raise their paw
When they want to go to the washroom.
Dogs that use their own basket to sleep in and pass
your best chair on the way without a glance.
Animals that can instruct
the littlest hobo in good manners.
Dogs that don't exist.

Or do they?

The Pet Store

You'll need to be on your best behaviour.
The dogs you find here are smart,
and not all that keen on leaving the shop.
They're well fed, have a warm shop to live in,
and plenty of their own kind of company.
Why would they want to leave with a complete stranger?
They have no idea of who you are or, more importantly,
where you've been.
So don't expect these dogs to put on a show for you.
You'll need to impress *them*.

Pretend you're interested in buying a goldfish.
Then add in a loud voice: "Although, frankly, the house
just cries out for a dog.
All those manicured lawns."
Describe in detail how James the Chauffeur
never misses a day asking you for a little doggy
to keep him company as he rambles over hill and dale.

Don't forget to mention your close friends who own
the gourmet pet store just down the street.
Ten minutes of this should have the store in an uproar.
Even the goldfish will be begging to leave.
One friend who tried this
ended up taking the shopkeeper
along with the dog.

Show Dogs

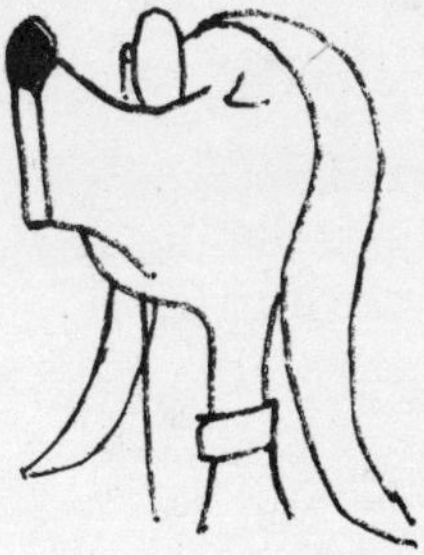

These are dogs with a past.
A past that any human
would be proud of.
And to prove it, the dog
comes
with a pedigree.
This does not mean
he wears nail polish.
It means he has breeding.
Breeding is the result of arranged marriages
between the aristocrats of the canine world.

No nipping across the street with any female that
comes around the corner.
It's a controlled affair.
Between dogs of the same size, shape, and colour.
But different sex.

Fully aware that their mating is being written down for posterity, these dogs keep their own mental diary:

Feb. 3

9:30 a.m. Blonde two-year old. Not bad if you like that kind of thing.

11:45 a.m. The blonde again. Boring.

2:45 a.m. Oh no, Not again. Wait a minute –
Boss dancing up and down
with the blonde's owner.
Blonde and I stop to watch.
Laugh ourselves silly.
They'll never get pregnant doing that.

Over afternoon tea the breeder will show you
the dog's complete history: who the dog's
mother was. Who *her* mother was. Who the sister of
her mother was. And who caused the black
spot to appear just behind all of their ears.
The further back this record goes,
the more you're going to pay.
So take your time.
Forget the scones and watercress sandwiches.
Watch carefully.

Will the puppies have the right shape ears for its breed?
Good enough to show in a ring?
Good enough to show out of a ring?
Only the blonde knows for sure.
You have taken a step that
will change your
life.

You have become a dog owner.
(You can now rescue a sagging conversation with:
"You'll never guess what . . . Fido did the other day"
. . . which will encourage the reply,
"If you think that's bad,
you should hear what Rover did last week.")
And what of the dog?

Those dogs who are just changing addresses
will do exactly what they did in
their old house . . . rule it.
For dogs going to a home for the first time
it won't be so easy.
It's going to take them time.
Time to look around.
Time to find out who
slyly drops bits from the dinner table.
Time to discover the best pieces of furniture.
Time to determine what will most irritate the neighbours.
It will take time to become top dog.
About one week.

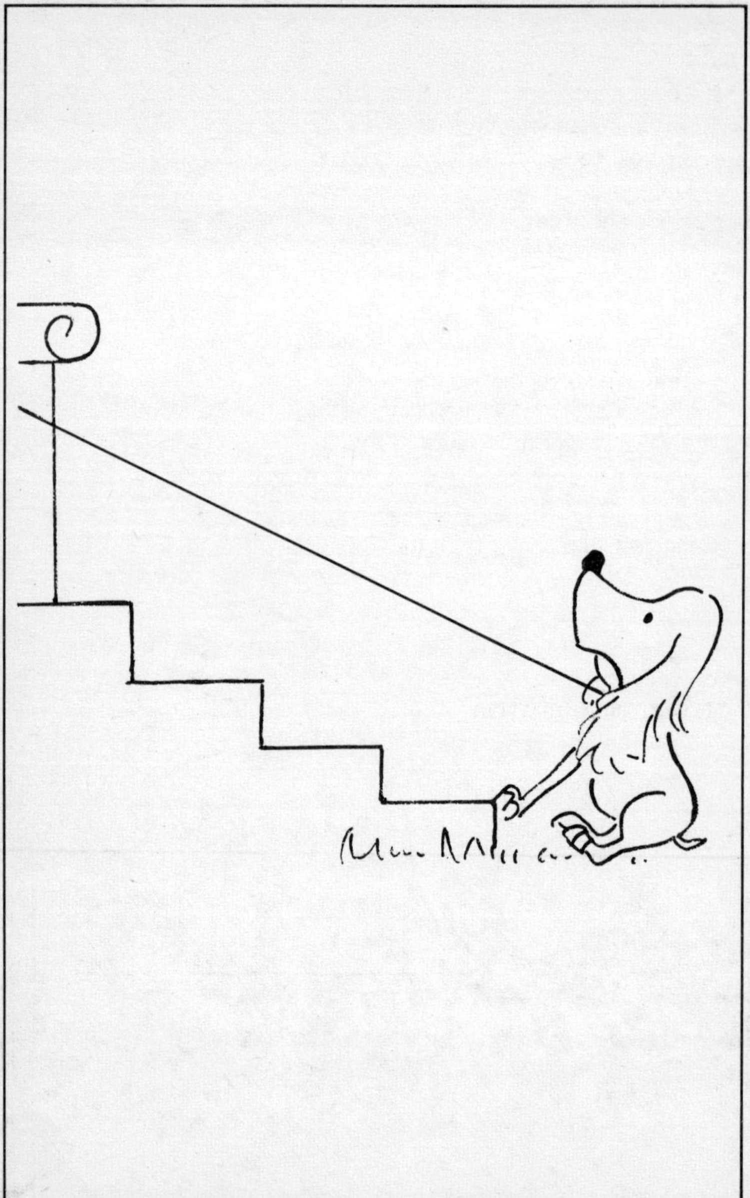

Owning a Dog

First Day Home

What was once your
home now belongs to
someone else.
You just pay the mortgage.

The first thing the new owner will want to do,
as you carry him across the threshold, is get down.
He has never been in the house before and will want to
reconnoitre the fridge and dining-room table.

After sniffing his way around the house he'll quickly
assess the area that you have set aside
for him.
He will then see that your area is infinitely better.
This is the beginning of the end.

House Breaking

Humans have long realized the
importance of toilet training.
Dogs have not.
Humans only visit the john
when it is necessary.
Not so the dog.
Nothing pleases a dog more than a tour
of animal comfort stations:
tree, fire hydrant, post.

Any outside upright objects.
And, unless the dog is well schooled,
every inside upright object
is treated as an outside upright object.
Chair legs are hydrants.
Table legs are hydrants.
Piano legs are hydrants.
And, if they stand still long enough,
human legs are hydrants.

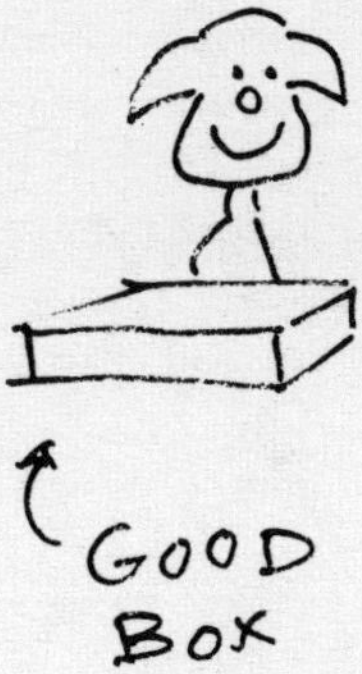

What you have to do
is convince the pup that a litter box
is really a hydrant.
This is no easy matter.
When you place him in the box,
he will climb out.
Since you're asking him to sit
on gravel, this should be no surprise.
But it is worth a try.
Speak to him gently.

Now pick him up and place him down in the box.
Stop him from leaving the box until you're
satisfied that he has used it properly.
Now pat him and tell him what a good boy he is.
Stand back as he runs to the piano leg.

But don't be too kind.
Puppies have been known to enjoy
the experience so much that they
have refused to leave the box for greener fields.
On the other hand, don't be too strict.
This has been known to permanently constipate dogs.
This may sound like the
ideal solution, but it makes a
dog cranky.

For older dogs other methods are
called for.

The most popular method
is newspaper training –
except among journalists.
First you'll need a newspaper.
A large one.
Several sections of it.
Ones you've read.
Lay the newspaper on the kitchen floor.
Why choose the place in the house
that contains the food?
For the simple reason that
wherever you place your newspaper,
your dog will choose somewhere else.

Once he has chosen somewhere else,
place another newspaper on that spot.
Your dog will soon catch on.
You will soon have the satisfaction
of seeing your dog use the newspaper
when Mother Nature calls.
But only when every square inch
of floor is covered in newspaper.

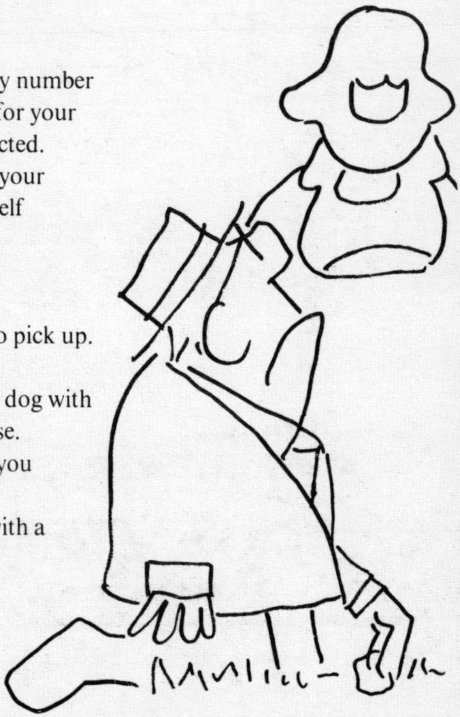

Although there are any number
of outside areas ideal for your
dog, they are all protected.
This is not to say that your
dog cannot avail himself
of the great outdoors.
But whatever
he leaves behind,
you will be expected to pick up.

Make sure to keep the dog with
you during this exercise.
If he gets out of sight you
may be taken for
a crackpot collector with a
weird hobby.

Fortunately ingenuity has stepped
in where men fear to tread.

Place over the stricken area
until passers-by have passed by.

Patented, Dec. 1982.
Serial number: 456289

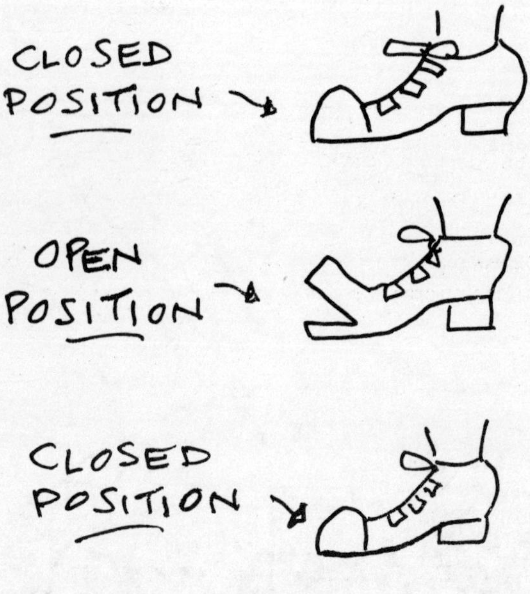

Patented, March 1983.
Serial Number: 497840984

Many readers are probably under the impression that
having a dog around the house is not a good idea.
Wrong.
Having a dog around the house is a wonderful idea.
But owners must make adjustments.
After all, wherever a dog walks around the house
a large pair of legs are in his way.
People insist on watching Dallas
regardless of the fact that the Littlest
Hobo, Rin Tin Tin, or Lassie are on another channel.
And worst of all, no one thinks of keeping the noise down
when he attempts to enjoy his favourite pastime . . .

Sleeping

Dogs love to sleep.
Dogs love to sleep anywhere.
Dogs love to sleep most of all where man sleeps.
From his first day in the house
your dog will search for
a better sleeping area
than the one he has
been allotted.
He knows there is one.
It's the room he is ordered
never to go into.
It's just a matter of time
until he gets inside.
What will he see?
A wide soft area covered with
clean sheets and two fluffy things
just waiting to be pushed around.

This is better than
the basement floor or a silly little
basket with a tiny blanket.
You'll need to be firm.
This is a territorial battle to the death.
"No! . . . Off! . . . Out!"
Then insist on at least one of the pillows.

It's morning. The first full day of your life
as a dog owner.
You have tried rocking the dog to sleep
You have tried rocking yourself to sleep.
You have been awake all night.

Don't be disheartened.
You have fifteen hours to go before
it's time for bed again.
Enjoy the day.
The dog will.

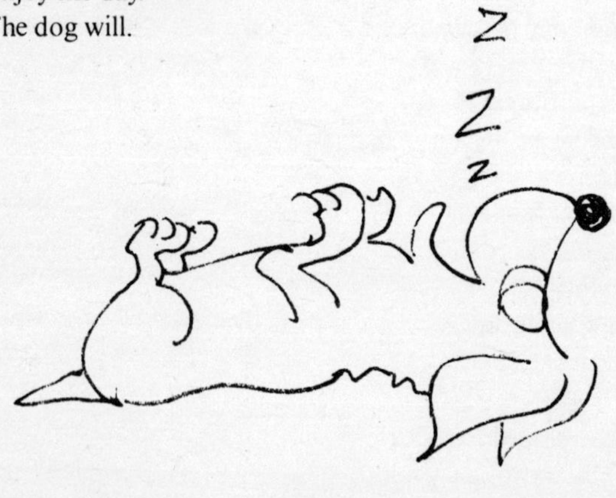

A Day in the Life of a Dog

6:00 a.m. – 6:15 a.m.	Squeals and whines to be let out of house.
6:16 a.m.	Rushes into garden in search of cats.
6:20 a.m.	No cats. Turns attention to newly planted bulbs.
6:21 a.m.	Digs up bulbs
6:30 a.m.	Barks to come inside.
6:32 a.m.	Barks again – more loudly.
6:35 a.m.	To be sure all within twenty miles have heard, barks again.
6:40 a.m.	Back door opens. Enters house. Listens to make sure everyone in house now awake. Jumps on chair and goes to sleep.
8:00 a.m.	Food sounds from kitchen. Wakes and goes to investigate. Hangs around chair of youngest human. Catches most food before it hits the floor.
8:32 a.m.	Back to sleep.
9:30 a.m.	Mail arrives. Waits for door to open and chases letter carrier.
9:45 a.m.	Sleep.
10:45 a.m.	Sleep.

11:00 a.m.	Vacuum cleaner switched on. Leaps from chair and flees sound. Goes to another room. Sleeps.
12:30 p.m.	Lunch sounds from kitchen. Scurries past newly filled dog dish. Arrives first at table. Waits for food to drop from table. None. Goes to dog dish filled with food the TV ad says is irresistible to dogs. Sniffs. Looks around to make sure there's nothing better. Sighs. Eats.

1:30 p.m.	Whines at door to go out.
1:35 p.m.	Whines at door to come in.
1:40 p.m.	Hears friend barking outside. Whines to go out again.
1:45 p.m.	Door opens. Leaps from house and joins friend chasing cars.
2:45 p.m.	Still chasing cars, with the odd cat thrown in for variety.
3:00 p.m.	Decides to call on girl-friend up the street. She is sleeping.
3:05 p.m.	Good idea. Goes home and does same.

4:00 p.m.	Children arrive home from school. Dog barks, yells, goes crazy. Told to calm down. Barks and yells some more.
4:07 p.m.	Grabbed by collar and thrown out of house.
4:09 p.m.	After loud barking fails to open door, decides to call on girl-friend once more. She has gone out. Runs to park. Finds another girl.

6:00 p.m.	Dinner time. Hurries home.
6:10 p.m.	Before door opens, lowers head and adopts pitiful appearance.
6:11 p.m.	Doesn't work. "Get in here and where the hell have you been?"
6:12 p.m.	Hides under dinner table.
6:55 p.m.	Hears rattle of leash. Leaps off best chair and rushes to front door.
7:17 p.m.	At the park. Leash still attached. Sits quietly. Leash released. Goes bananas.
7:55 p.m.	Off leash.
8:22 p.m.	Off leash.
8:55 p.m.	Off leash.

9:15 p.m.	Owner asks if anyone has seen a dog.
9:45 p.m.	Owner in luck. Someone has seen a dog swimming in nearby lake.
10:00 p.m.	Back on leash. Shakes self over owner.

10:05 p.m.	Dragged back into house.
10:15 p.m.	Settles down in front of TV.
10:35 p.m.	Barks to go outside.
10:40 p.m.	Barks loudly to come back inside.

10:45 p.m.	Barks again before owner can open door. Neighbour shouts that baby is trying to sleep. Also advises what owner should do with dog.
10:46 p.m.	Dog barks very loudly in the direction of neighbour's voice.
10:50 p.m.	Door opens. Dog rushes upstairs to bedroom. Hides under bed. Owner leaves. Dog leaps onto bed. Sleeps.

Our Daily Breed

From the events of your first day
together you will discover that
what you command and what the dog does
are two different things.

This is because there is a language
barrier between humans and dogs.

If you feel that you
and the dog
should understand each other,
you are the one who will have to adapt.

Here are a few simple phrases to start you off:

English	*Dog Translation*
Up	Down
Down	Up
Sit	Stand
Stand	Sit

It's not that the dog
does not want to please.
Far from it.
But a certain physical happening
deep in the middle ear
reverses
whatever you command your dog to do.

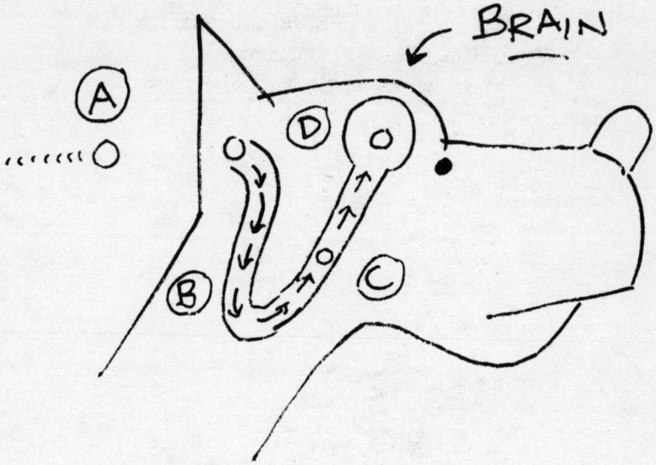

(A) Word "Stay."

(B) Word travels into the ear.

(C) Word forced to reverse direction.

(D) Arrives at brain. Word now reversed. "Stay" is now "Come."

But the true marvel of the dog's brain is shown at mealtime, when two senses work as one. The words "Come and get it" cause the ears to lift to their fullest extent. At the same time, the smell of food hitting the nostrils causes an emergency trapdoor to open in the extended ears, bypassing all other channels. For the first time A to D is the shortest distance between two points.

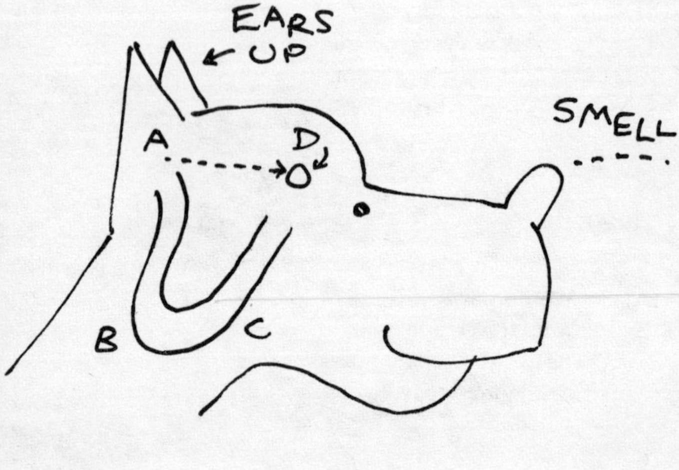

Feeding

There are many dog foods on the market.
Some are good.
Some are bad.
Which should you buy?
It doesn't matter.
He'll ignore them all and
eat only what
you're eating.

"Eating" is not quite accurate.
Inhaling would be nearer the truth.
Whatever the size of the portion,
in it goes
never to appear again.
Why does he do this?
It saves time, for one thing.
He's also bored.
He has little to occupy his mind
Doesn't read.
Dislikes television.
And since he is the only dog
in the house, there is little love interest.

One of the wonders of nature is
the way that a dog's mouth, large or small, will
be able to accommodate any amount of food.
How is this possible?
By a remarkable piece of machinery:

The smell of food
hits the nose.
Nose twitches (A).

Nose twitch activates
mouth mechanism (B).

Muscle
disengages itself
from upper jaw (C).

Lower jaw drops.
Tunnel now ready
to take in supplies (D).

Unfortunately for the dog,
nothing in his
body tells him
when he has had enough.
If your dog finds it easier
to roll than walk,
he is eating too much.

You can do one or both of two things.
1. Exercise the dog;
2. Put him on a diet.

Exercise:

Move his food dish as far away as possible
from where he sleeps.
When you are going out for a drive take him
along . . . trotting behind the car.

There is one problem.
Exercise tends to give your dog an appetite.

Diet:

Stop feeding your dog.
Not forever. Just a little while.
This will not be easy.
Every time you eat,
the dog will make you feel guilty.
Some owners have stopped eating entirely.
This just informs the dog that there
is more than the usual amount of food in the fridge.

Before you start on your dog's diet make sure you know the size you want to end up with. To take ten pounds off a dog that weighs nine can be detrimental to the dog's health. To help you determine your dog's ideal consult the chart below:

Size	Weight
	385 pounds
	10 ounces

Once you have started the diet,
stick to your guns.
The dog has ways of enticing food from
the tightest human fist.

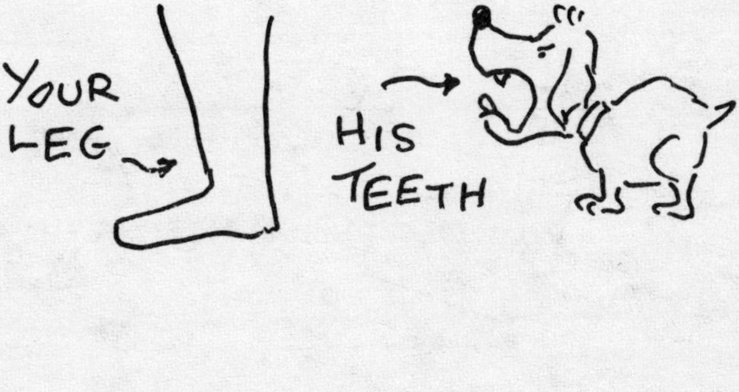

Sex

To a dog, all members of the opposite
sex look the same.
Blonde, redhead, or brunette, it doesn't matter.
If he's in the mood,
away he goes.
Unfortunately, unless the female is in heat
she couldn't care less.
As a result, male dogs turn their attention
to other sex objects.
Sexy can be anything that moves.
And many things that don't move.
So if your dog appears to be in love with the leg
of your Louis XIV chair, don't panic.
It's his way of saying he loves you.
But he loves the furniture more.
If playing second fiddle to an antique upsets you,
get your dog fixed.
It's best for you.
It's best for the neighbourhood.
It's best for the dog.
And it's best for the furniture.

Sickness

Dogs get sick like anyone else.
Unfortunately (for them) they can't tell you about it.
So how do you know?
When you open the door to take him to the park
and he prefers to stay in the house,
he is not feeling well.
Take him to the vet.

But don't tell him where he's going.
He won't want to go.
And he will know where you're taking him. So there's no
point pretending you're going to the park.
Be honest.
"Out of the
chair.
We're off
to get you a
nice big
needle."
Better to have the fuss at home in private than
in the vet's office where everyone will watch.

Once you're at the vet's,
look for the quietest dog in the waiting-room.
Make sure it is still breathing.
Ask its name.
"Look at Gertrude sitting all quiet.
She's getting a big fat needle and
she's not crying about it."

Almost every dog disease
is prevented or cured by a needle.
"It's a cold, Mr. Wicks, we'll give him a shot."
"It's a sore foot, Mr. Wicks, we'll give him a shot."
"It's distemper, Mr. Wicks, we'll give him a shot."
"Here's the bill for the shots, Mr. Wicks."
"Quick, nurse – catch Mr. Wicks.
We'll give him a shot."

Baths

Next to the vet, the thing dogs hate
most is a bath.
And for a very good reason.
They figure they smell great just as they are.
In fact, they can't get enough
of each other's smell.
The worse a dog smells,
the better his social life.
So remember that
you bathe your dog
for you, not for him.

Getting him into the tub is tricky.
Put the water in first.
Warm water is ideal.
Whistle and sing as the tub fills.
Give the impression that you are about to have a great time.
Talk to the dog.
This will help to divert his attention from the sound of running water.

Help him to relax.
"Doggy going for swimmsy?" is good for openers.
(If your dog sinks like a stone, this is not good for openers.)

Roll up your trousers
or hitch up your dress and step into the
tub to show him how wonderful it is.
(He has a right to know it's safe.)
Laugh, giggle, and sing as you wriggle your toes in the tub.
Play with his rubber ducks and cats.
Splash a little water his way.
Not too much or he will feel
that he is already in the bath.

If he still refuses
to get into the tub,
pick him up and drop him in.

Travelling With Your Dog

Bored with hanging around the house,
a dog cannot wait to get
away from it.
The further, the better.
If you thought a dog
got excited at going
for a walk, wait until
you take him for a
car ride.
Here is the chance
to really get away.
And not just to some silly old park.
The car means countryside
and scenery.
Allow him to get inside the car first.
Close the doors.
Give him a chance to settle down.
After forty-five minutes, it's safe
to get in with him.

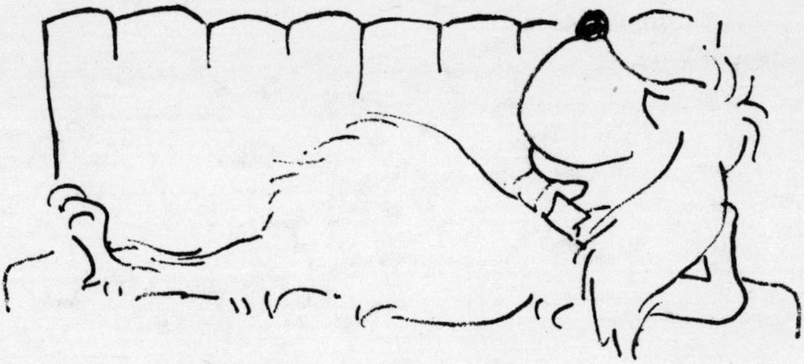

Take a seat the dog isn't in.
(Unless he's taken over the driver's seat.)
Since he has four legs, the dog will naturally feel that he should be allotted two seats.
(Humans, two legs = one seat.
Dogs, four legs = two seats.)
You can change his mind by having the heaviest member of the party sit on one of the two seats he is occupying.

You are now ready to start . . . .

Unless the dog is about to get sick.
This should not happen
if the dog
has been denied food
for at least
two hours
before the trip.
However, it will happen.

The causes for car sickness are many.
Maybe it's your driving.
Are people carsick when you drive?
If only your dog suffers,
maybe the cause is static electricity.
It's nature's way of telling us we should all
travel by horse-drawn cart.
For those interested in the
phenomenon of static electricity I have
prepared an explanatory chart.
Since it is extremely technical, and most
readers will find it beyond their understanding,
I am publishing it separately.

Without getting too technical,
here's what happens.
Static electricity is all over the place.
(Since all matter consists of atoms and each of these have electrons, you can imagine how much of the stuff is around.
The wonder is that we don't get carsick all the time.)
Atoms full of electrons and protons (A) are suddenly attracted toward a car (B).
Its rubber tires (C) rub against the road gathering static electricity.

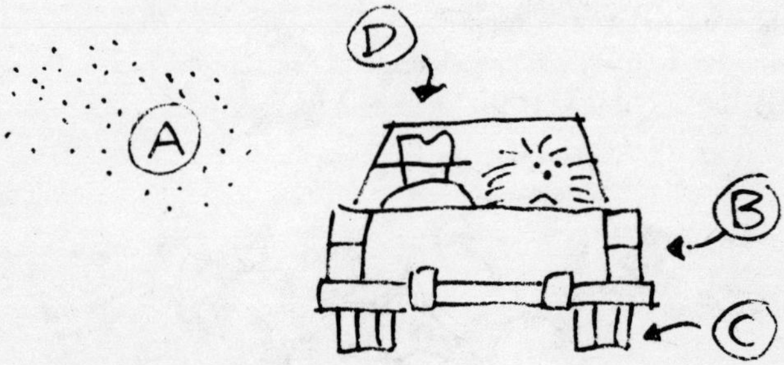

This load of static electricity then jumps into the car and starts whirling around inside.
Who's going to get it?
The one most like a carpet —
the dog (D).
The poor dog is so bombarded by all these electrons that eventually he's sick.
(We all know how we can get shocks from a carpet when we touch a doorknob.

This is why a dog never opens a door
by touching the door handle.)
What can you do about static electricity?
Divert it somewhere else.
Hang a piece of chain from the rear bumper
so it touches the road.
The static electricity hitting your car
will travel along the chain to the road.
It will then hit the car behind whose driver has not
had the good sense to hang a piece of chain
from the rear bumper.

You will know when the dog is about to be sick.
He will drool or swallow rapidly.
Stop the car as quickly as possible.
Get the dog out of the car. . . .
Not soon enough.

You'll need to stop at the nearest gas station to
clean up thoroughly.

If you are in need of gas approach the pumps carefully. The dog is not feeling all that great, and the sight of a man dressed like a mailman can be the last straw.

Try not to roll down your window to speak to the attendant.
Use sign language.
Make sure your hands do not wander toward the dog.
The only thing that's going to make him forget the pain he's feeling is if someone else shares it.
And when you've filled up and you're driving away, don't feel too bad.
Your dog will probably not be sick again for another hour.

Railways and airlines insist on your dog
being out of hearing and out of sight of others.
This is an admirable arrangement.
You will not be humiliated in front of the passengers
in first class.
You will be handed a container to place
your dog in.
Make sure it's the right size.

If you are not happy with the
container, say so.
Since many of the countries you're going to couldn't
care less whether your dog comes in or not, he won't
need a passport.

However, in some places, they assume the dog is your lunch.
If you do not fancy Fido, put a sign around his neck.
This will not guarantee he will not become someone else's lunch, but it may slow them down long enough for you to claim him in the baggage area.

Warning:
Foreign dogs are not safe in Britain!
This island of dog lovers will immediately grab yours and imprison him for six months.
Despite your dog pleading that he has never felt better.
It seems to work.
The English claim they have had no rabies since Henry VIII, and even he had only a mild case.

Who's in Charge Here?

There's no turning back.
You've got your best friend.
But how long will the friendship last?
As with all relationships you're going to have to learn to give and take:
Give the dog what he wants and take him to the park.
You are no longer the master of your own home.
Your life is ruled by a dog.
The only thing you can do is keep it a secret.
This can only be done by getting the dog to behave in such a way as to give the impression that you're the boss.
How do you get your dog to do what you want him to do?
It's not easy.
Look at it from the dog's point of view.
A strange-looking being standing on two of its four legs is giving orders.
Instead of barking, this weirdo is using a foreign language.
Besides, most of the orders are ridiculous.
The dog is told to sit when he isn't tired.
Told to stand when he's exhausted.
To lie down when he's ready to walk and walk when he wants to sleep.
Give your dog a chance.

Teach him to understand what it is you
want him to do.
Then he can refuse.

Getting Him To Understand

Many owners try shouting,
jumping up and down, standing on their
heads or demonstrating what they
want their dog to do.
Most dogs sense that this owner is off his
rocker and join in the fun by barking
and jumping all over him.
Dogs that worry about what the neighbours will say
decide that a trot back to the house is preferable
to being seen in the company of this lunatic.
So let's start at the beginning.

Stay calm.

Training

The best time to start training is when the dog is between seven and twelve weeks.
At this time his personality is being formed.
The angry dog of the future can be taught that you mean business when you tell him to let go of the mailman's behind.
Unless the dog gets all the mail.
It's the best time for the dog to get accustomed to the sound of the human voice.

If the dog is shy, you can help bring him out.
If he's stubborn he can learn that you are not happy when he leaves the park to cross a highway in a search of better company.
The key is to keep up regular training.
The beauty of working with your dog is that you will need no tools other than those you already have.
A voice. A hand. A heart.
And patience.

The Voice

Whether it's high, low, or can carry a tune it's
the tone of the voice that the dog will understand.
He's not understanding the words.
He's understanding the way they're spoken.
(Just as you do when you don't tip a cab driver enough.)

Up

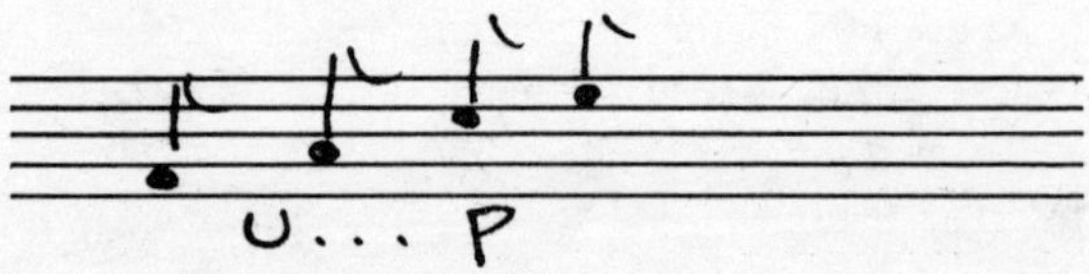

Down

Lie

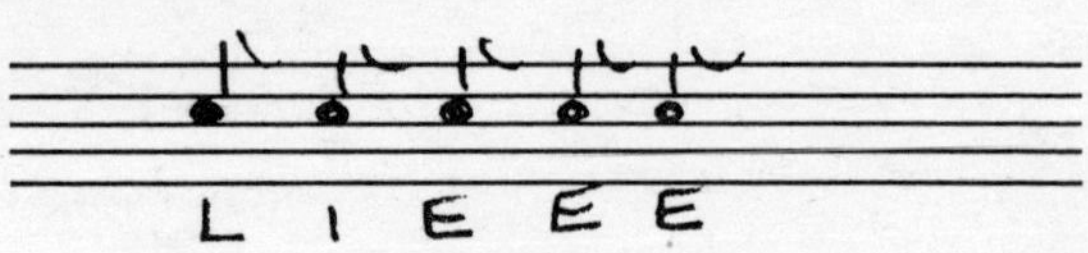

Stay

The Hand

You'll need the hand to demonstrate.
Press on his rear. He will soon learn that sitting
is more comfortable than holding up
your weight and his.
This is also more comfortable for you
than sitting in the middle of a damp park
to show the dog what "Sit" means.

If a crowd gathers and begins to laugh,
laugh with them.
They will think that what
your dog is doing is part of your plan.
Or cause a diversion:
Throw a stick and in a loud voice cry "Fetch!"
The dog will not bring the stick back.
But it will sway public opinion.
The crowd will think that the dog is the idiot.

Whatever you do, don't lose patience.
Look at it from the dog's point of view.
Whenever he brings you the stick
you just throw it away again.
There's always another day.
Go home and relax.
One other thing:
take the dog with you.

You can try out a few orders in the house,
but sooner or later you'll have to take your dog outside.
There the dog will have the space and
the excuses he needs to
disobey.
"You'll have to talk louder. I was too far away to hear you."
"I wanted to do what you asked but another dog
was talking to me at the time."
So be prepared.
Before you leave the house tell the dog
what lesson you will be giving him.
"Today we're going to learn 'Heel.' Do you hear me?"
If he nods his head
you're ready to start.
How many of us have witnessed the
pathetic attempts by most humans to
take their dog for a walk?

Little old ladies dragged to parks they
had no intention of visiting.
Little old men being dragged to
the same parks only to find themselves
colliding with the little old ladies at
every tree stop.

You must be in command.
You'll need a collar and a leash.
Make sure the dog is on one end and
you're on the other.
If it's his first time out,
he'll want to show you
the neighbourhood.
He will need to know
which end of the leash is in charge.
It's the end with the heels, not the paws.
Remind him each time he
gets ahead of you:
"Heel. . . . Heel. . . ."

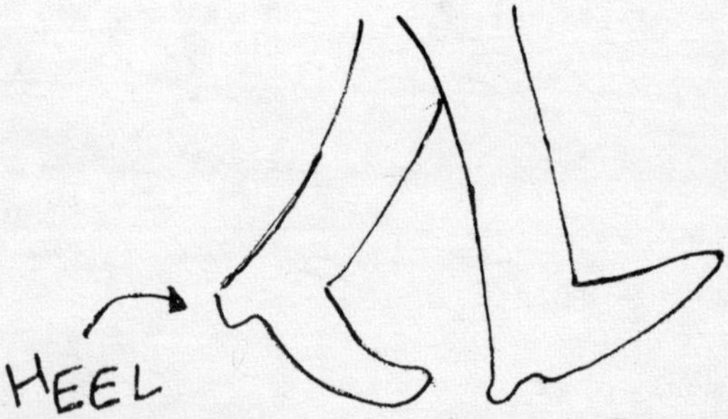

Heel

It's the most important
command of all.
And the toughest.
It's the command given when you want
your dog to trot at your side and
never get in front of you.
Though why this concept should be
understood by dogs when simple words
like "sit" are beyond them
is beyond me.
Nevertheless, it's worth a try.
Whenever he feels that the fire hydrant
across the street is more important than
walking at your heel,
get down to his level
and look him in the eye.
"If you keep this up, we're
going home. Do you understand?"
His tail will wag, showing that he
hasn't the faintest idea.

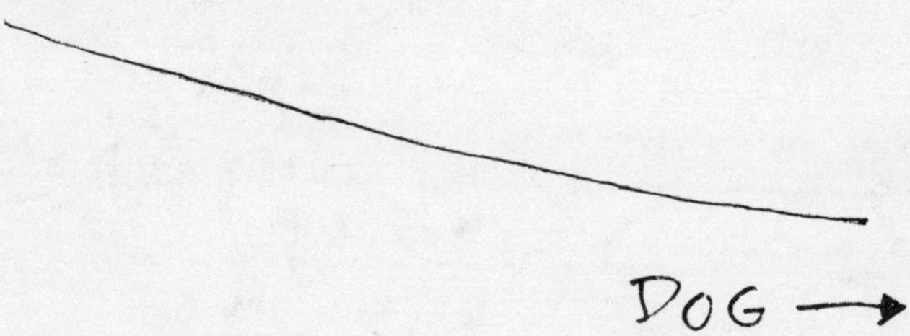

Go

In the park you will need a long piece of rope. And the dog.

A good length for the rope is fifty feet. That's long enough for you to fool the dog into thinking he is free. It's also short enough for the dog to hear what you scream at him.

EH?

A wide open space is good.
Well away from lakes and ponds.
Especially if your dog
is quite strong.

Make it easy for yourself.
Pick a place with few distractions.
Other dogs, especially those of the other
persuasion, can have a disastrous effect
on even the best training period.
Start with something easy to get you in the
right frame of mind.
Lower your dog to the ground
Grip the collar.
Whisper in his ear "Go!"
Release the collar.
Now. How about that? Your dog has now screeched away.
At least for a distance of fifty feet.

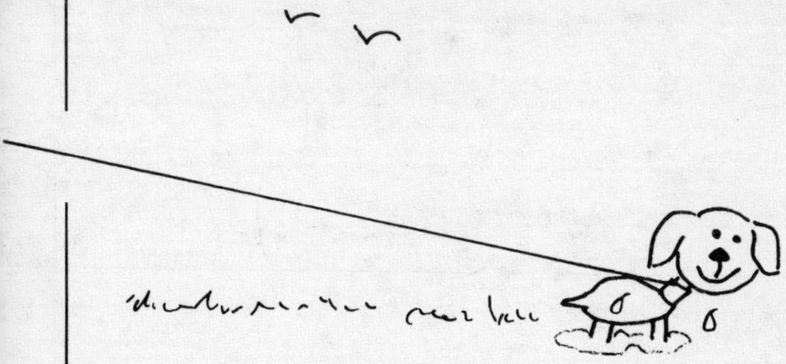

Make sure your feet are firmly on the ground
to absorb the tremendous jolt
on your end of the rope.
Your dog is now upside down,
three feet off the ground.

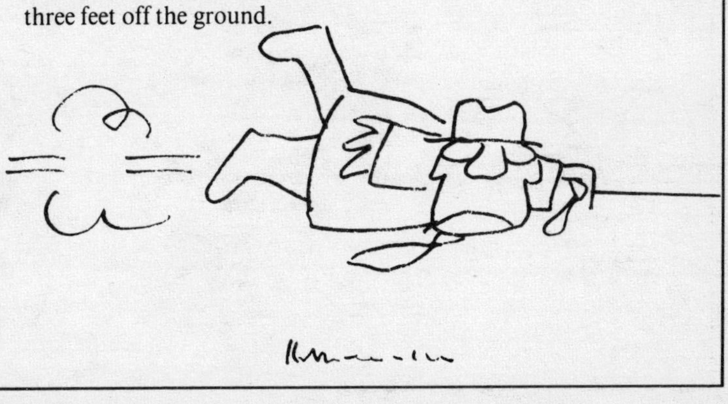

You have just successfully completed
lesson one.
You have given your
dog the order to go and he
has obeyed.

Come

Now comes the difficult part.
How to get him to come back.
The use of more than one word will confuse him.
"Come" is the word you need. (Not "back.")
After the rope incident he
is not in a very good mood.

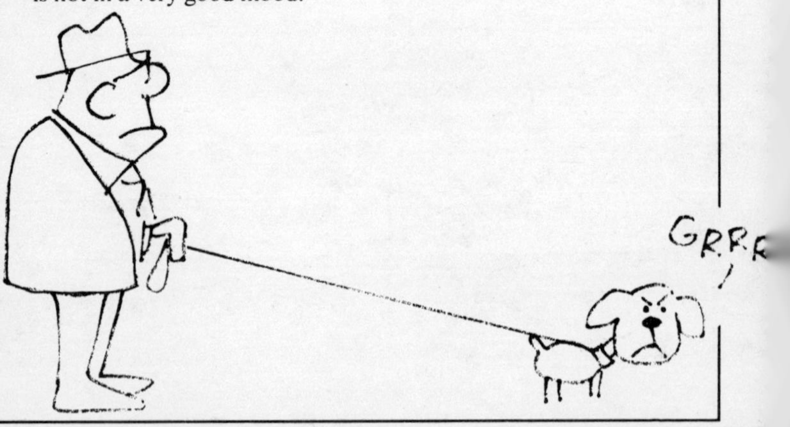

Smile.
"Hi there, old buddy."
Don't ask him how he's been. The memory of near strangulation is still fresh in his mind.
Avoid, "You'll never guess what I've got for you."
The dog may feel that what you have for him is more of the same.

Play it safe.
"Want to have some fun, boy?"

Is he wagging his tail?
Good. He has heard what you said and forgotten about the rope.

You are now ready to use the word.
Remember to keep smiling.
Now get ready.
Not too loud.
"Come."

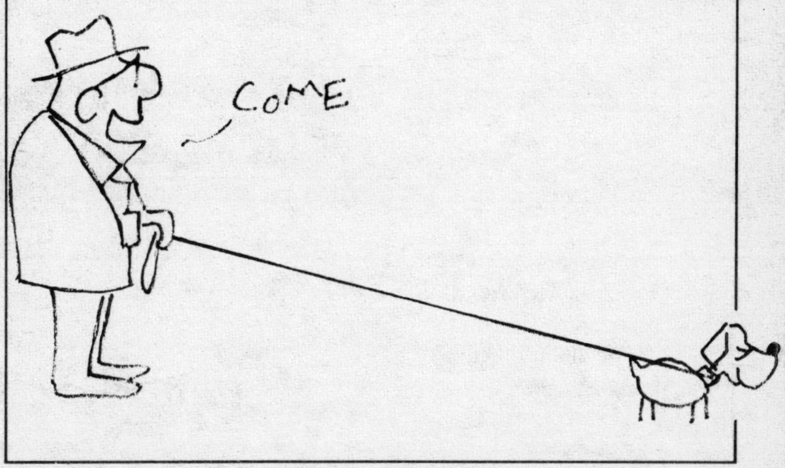

Try again . . . a little louder.
"Come."
Keep smiling.
"Come."
Is he still wagging his tail?
Maybe the rope incident has left him a little deaf.

Try a little louder.
"COME."

Follow along the rope and scream in his ear.
"C . . . O . . . M . . . E."

You may feel that the dog has made no progress.
He has.
He has broken through the
language barrier with the human.
You shouted, "Come."
And you did just that.

Stay

So the dog refused to move when you asked him to "Come." Improvise. Tell him you want him to stay where he is.

Place the dog on the ground.

Lift a finger (yours). Point it at the dog.

In a firm voice say . . .
"STAY."

Now slowly back away, repeating as you do, "STAY."
Keep your eyes on the dog's face.

Back up carefully.
To fall over at this point would ruin everything.
Repeat "STAY" every ten paces.

When you are fifty feet away give one last shout.
"STAY!"

So he loves you so much that he can't
bear to be away from you.
Is that bad?

Sit

There is no finer sight
than that of a proud
owner telling a dog
to sit – and he does.
You, too, can teach your
dog to sit.

However, most dogs prefer to lie.
With four legs, one
in each corner,
sitting is a little
awkward.
The two front legs
take all the weight
in the sitting position.
The back two just
spread along the floor.

So if you do manage to
get your dog to sit in
public, quickly follow
the command, "Sit,"
with "Lie."
Some owners tread on a
dog's tail to make him sit.
This method does
get the dog's attention, but I would
advise against such an action.
Especially with large dogs.
If all else fails,
if the dog absolutely refuses to do
what you ask,
don't despair.
There are others who will take over where you left off.

Obedience School

Dogs are like children.
Some are smart.
Some are not.

Smart dogs lie around the house all day.
They are seen but not heard.
Their walks consist of a trot
at their master's heel interrupted only
by the occasional comfort stop.
These dogs are few.
And old. Very old.
Most people have dogs that
are young, frisky, and dumb.
Therefore they are impossible to train.
Except by experts.
There are now thousands of obedience schools spotted
around the globe.
All with one aim.
To teach your dog good manners.

Most schools are split into three grades.
Quick learners, slow learners, and
a waste of money.
Once you have decided on the school, pay it a visit.
Do not be surprised if the person you meet at the
school is covered with scars and bites.
The trainer's nerves will be shot. He will twitch.
He will give you a form to fill in.
Here is a sample:

Obedience School   Form 8674B   Photo of Your Dog

Name of Dog: ______________________

Address: ______________________

Size: ( ) Bigger than a bread box   ( ) Smaller than a bread box

Has your dog ever been in trouble with the law? ( ) Yes ( ) No

If yes, what was the charge? ( ) Biting ( ) Theft ( ) Murder

Does your dog have a prison/pound record?

Has your dog ever attacked anyone? ( ) Yes ( ) No

If yes, how many times?

Is the victim still living? ( ) Yes ( ) No

If "no," was the demise the result of the attack?

Does your dog chase ( ) cars ( ) cats ( ) mailmen ( ) anything that moves?

Does he make friends easily? ( ) Yes ( ) No

Does he make enemies easily? ( ) Yes ( ) No

Medical History: ______________________

____

____

____

____

Will you be able to pay the fee ( ) Now ( ) Later today ( ) Early tomorrow

Consent Form:

I . . . . agree that whatever the school decides is best for my dog they have my consent to do it. This includes expulsion at any time of the day or night.

If it is not possible to teach my dog anything, I want him:
( ) Brought home ( ) Sent to another school
( ) Set loose close to the pound

The school will want to know as much as possible about your dog.
Often, like humans, a dog reveals his feelings in his face.
For this reason many schools have a second form that you will be asked to complete.
It will look something like the following:

Dog's Name:

Address:

Birth Date: Breed:

Sire (Father) Dame (Mother)

Sex Colour Markings

Weight Height Length Ears (How Many) Eyes (How Many)

Distinguishing Features:

....

My dog looks like this when he is happy:

( ) ( ) ( )

My dog looks like this when he is unhappy:

( ) ( ) ( )

My dog looks like this all the time:

( ) ( ) ( )

....

How would you describe your financial situation.

( ) Comfortable ( ) I manage ( ) Desperate

Once your dog has been accepted by the school
he will be taken by his teacher to the
exercise area.
Here he will receive his first lessons
from a muscular man who has obviously
seen the inside of a lion's mouth.

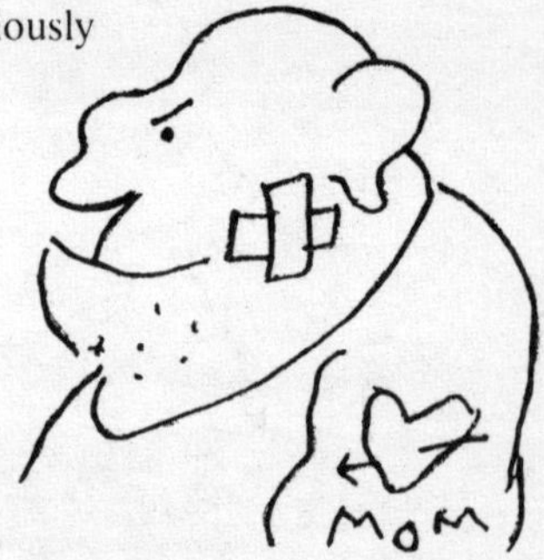

The large man will smile
warmly and crack his whip.
The moment the dog obeys he will
be rewarded with a cookie.
Few cookies are given out
during the first two weeks.

Some schools prefer to teach
more than one dog at a time.

A previously graduated dog
is hidden in the group.
Unaware that they are watching a graduate,
the other dogs try hard for fear
of appearing stupid.
It also encourages the staff.
When they tell twenty dogs to sit,
they can count on
one to obey.

On graduation day a short speech to the
proud dog owners is usually followed
by a controlled walk around the yard with
teacher and dog in perfect harmony.
The dogs are then handed
over to their owners,
who also receive
a small scroll
attesting to the fact that
the dog has passed,
and that you have paid.

The scroll should be framed and placed
over your best chair. Your dog will get many a
good laugh every time he jumps into the chair to sleep.
You are the proud owner of the kind of dog
people marvel at in the movies.
A dog that will untie you if you are ever tied up
by a gang of bank robbers.
A dog that will leap over a high building
to knock a person from his horse.
A dog that will gather two hundred sheep together,
force them to swim a wide river, and battle their way
through a forest fire before placing them in three ranks
outside the ranch-house door.
You are the proud owner of a dog that you wish to show others.

Showing Your Dog

A dog show is a beauty contest.
Your dog will not be asked to
sing or play the piano.
It's for good-lookers only.
And there's plenty of them.
All with faces like Bo Derek
or Paul Newman.

Getting into a dog show is no big deal.
Just pay your money and in you go.
For $50 and a six-hour wait in a hall
filled with the stench of 2000 dogs,
you'll get a ten-cent piece of ribbon.

Ribbons do not mean a bag of beans to the dog.
He is there because you took him there.
If he had his way, he'd be in the nearest
park chasing a squirrel up a tree.
All the dog gets is nervous.

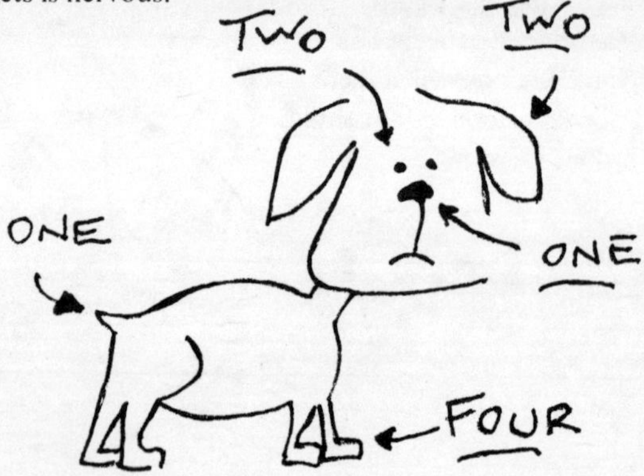

The judges will need to
get a close look at your dog
to make sure that he has
everything that he is
supposed to have.
During this examination your
dog will be expected to
stand perfectly still.
This is no easy task.
Leaning on the dog's head (if it is a big dog) or
placing a foot on the dog's head (if it is a small dog)
is not allowed.
The good news is that the owner beside you
is also expected to keep his dog still.
A good sharp cough at the right time can do wonders.

The Judge

Unlike a real judge,
a dog judge is paid
a pittance and needs
very little experience.
Since all dogs look alike,
the judges look for the things
any idiot can spot.

Typical Judge's Card

Dog Points

Name of Dog:			
Number of Legs:			
Number of Eyes:			
Number of Ears:			
Teeth ( ) Yes ( ) No		Awake ( )Yes ( ) No.	
Dead ( ) Yes ( ) No		Not sure ( )	

How then is one dog judged over another?
It isn't.
The owner and handler is.

How you behave toward the judge
is what wins ribbons.
A wink or a smile can do wonders.
A "well done, Judge" as he leaves can do even more.

Don't be afraid to offer to help.
The judge has been standing
for up to ten hours.
Tell him to take a weight off his feet.
You'll be happy to take over and judge
your own dog.
He will refuse.
But he won't forget you and your offer.
As he leaves to judge another dog, a hearty "Bye, Judge,
and thanks again for everything," should do the trick.
You'll probably need a wheel barrow
to take home the ribbons.

The Twilight Years

We all grow old.
A dog is no different.
What was once a nearby glorious park filled with sticks to fetch is now a field miles away up the street filled with tree branches too heavy to lift.
If you've grown old together, the arrangement is just fine.
You're too old to throw and he's too old to fetch.
If the dog has aged faster than you have
during the course of your relationship,
be patient.
A dog becomes hard of
hearing the same as we do.
When you ask him if he'd
like to go for a walk and
he ambles to his food dish,
repeat what you said.
This time show him his leash.
From close in.
He could also be a little
short-sighted.

Don't walk him too far.
What to your old pal was once
a skip and a jump
has now become a marathon.
The park down the end of the street
is a major expedition.
So take your time.

He wants to go to the park
but is now old enough to figure
that if he takes an hour to get there
it won't have gone anywhere.

When it's time for home,
he may need a carry.
If he's large, take a friend.
If he's too large
take a family.
And if you're still having trouble,
take a truck.

So if you can't see the fire, move your chair.
If his snores are too loud, turn up the television.
If he has rolled over onto your feet and they've gone
numb, move them carefully so as not to disturb him.
The silly bundle of fur that you brought to the
house so many years ago has seen a lot and done a lot —
mostly things you didn't want him to do.
Well it's too late to start teaching him now.
Relax.
Sit back and enjoy him.
It's still his house.
And don't you forget it.

There is lots more I wanted to
write about dogs.
But Rosie feels I've said enough.
Okay, okay . . . I'm coming Rosie.
Just sit quietly.
I'll take you for your walk
as soon as I fin . . . .